Eleanor Roosevelt

Eleanor Roosevelt

ACTIVIST FOR SOCIAL CHANGE

ALLISON LASSIEUR

FRANKLIN WATTS
A Division of Scholastic Inc.
New York Toronto London Auckland Sydney
Mexico City New Delhi Hong Kong
Danbury, Connecticut

For Hannah and Alyssa

All Photographs © 2007: AP/Wide World Photos: 68, 72; Corbis Images: 9, 34, 41, 43, 44, 46, 50, 58, 66, 80, 88, 93, 96 (Bettmann), 40, 90 (Hulton-Deutsch Collection), 24 (Notman Photo Co.), cover portrait (Sylvia Salmi/Bettmann), cover background (Joseph Sohm/Visions of America), 52 (Underwood & Underwood), 2, 6, 12, 49, 64, 75; Franklin D. Roosevelt Library: 14, 16, 18, 22, 28, 31, 37, 38, 56, 60, 62, 78; Getty Images: 86 (Fox Photos/Hulton Archive), 84 (George Silk/Time Life Pictures).

Library of Congress Cataloging-in-Publication Data
Lassieur, Allison.
  Eleanor Roosevelt : Activist for Social Change / by Allison Lassieur.
      p. cm. — (Great life stories)
  Includes bibliographical references and index.
  ISBN-10: 0-531-13871-2 (lib. bdg.)   0-531-17846-3 (pbk.)
  ISBN-13: 978-0-531-13871-7 (lib. bdg.)   978-0-531-17846-1 (pbk.)
  1. Roosevelt, Eleanor, 1884–1962—Juvenile literature. 2. Presidents' spouses—United States—Biography—Juvenile literature. I. Title. II. Series.
  E807.1.R48L384 2006
  973.917'092—dc22   2005024263

Published in 2007 by Franklin Watts, an imprint of Scholastic Library Publishing.
All rights reserved. Published simultaneously in Canada.
Printed in Mexico.

FRANKLIN WATTS and associated logos are trademarks and/or registered trademarks
of Scholastic Library Publishing. SCHOLASTIC and associated logos are trademarks
and/or registered trademarks of Scholastic Inc.

1 2 3 4 5 6 7 8 9 10 R 16 15 14 13 12 11 10 09 08 07

Contents

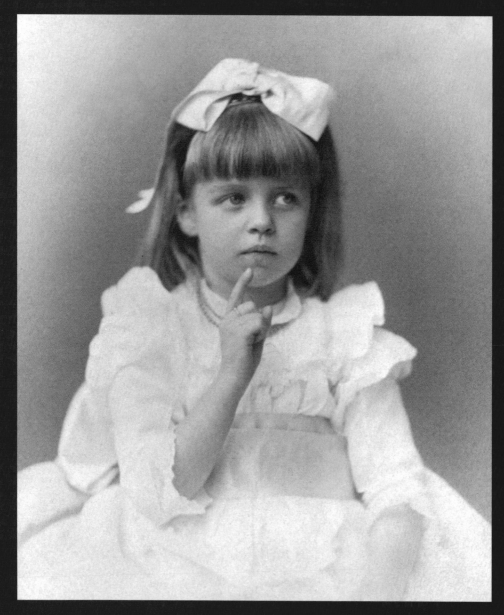

Eleanor's early years were full of turmoil and tragedy.

ONE

A Golden World

Of all the American women who have influenced history, none has been so admired, and so detested, as Eleanor Roosevelt. She was an outspoken feminist at a time when women's rights were discouraged. She promoted tolerance and respect for all races when hatred of black Americans ran deep. She worked tirelessly to improve the living conditions of the poorest Americans while facing criticism from her enemies.

But Eleanor Roosevelt didn't begin as such a strong, outspoken crusader. She was born at a time when women were valued more for their looks and money than for their intelligence. She was a quiet, shy child. Her early life was marked by depression, sadness, and terrible tragedy.

SECRETS BENEATH THE GLITTER

In the 1800s, the wide streets of New York City were lined with stately homes and townhouses owned by the wealthiest people in America. These residents' days were filled with shopping and luncheons. There was a party almost every evening. Families vacationed at their country homes far away from the hot city.

Anna Hall and Elliott Roosevelt lived in this rich and glittering world. They would one day become Eleanor's parents.

"ONE OF THE MOST BEAUTIFUL WOMEN"

Eleanor's mother, Anna Rebecca Livingston Ludlow Hall, was a striking beauty. Eleanor would later write, "My mother was one of the most beautiful women I have ever seen." Anna's father, Valentine Hall, had strict ideas about how family should behave. Valentine did not allow his wife, Mary, or his daughters to educate themselves. They could only pursue interests such as music, religion, a bit of literature, and other feminine pastimes. They were forbidden to handle money or to shop in public. He believed that his girls must have straight posture, so he ordered Anna and her sister Elizabeth to hike for hours with sticks held across their shoulders by the crooks of their elbows.

When Anna was seventeen, Valentine died suddenly. For the first time, there was no one to rule the Hall family. Mary had no idea how to run a household. Anna's two brothers, Valentine and Edward, were twelve and eight years old. Her younger sisters, Edith and Maude, were seven and three. The children became uncontrollable.

Anna tried to rein in her brothers and sisters, but she resented the position that she had been forced into. Anna longed to return to her old life, where she was the center of attention.

"CHARMING, GOOD-LOOKING, LOVED BY ALL"

Her chance came in the form of a handsome, dashing young man named Elliott Roosevelt. Eleanor described her father as "charming, good-looking, loved by all who came in contact with him." His father, Theodore Sr., was different from other wealthy men. He was concerned with the plight of the poor and the homeless. Theodore Sr. helped to found many New York charities, including the Children's Aid Society, hospitals, and the Society for the Prevention of Cruelty to Animals. He was devoted to his children: Theodore Jr., Elliott, Anna, and Corinne.

Elliott was the child everyone loved. As a boy, he was confident and outgoing. However, when he was fourteen, he began to suffer from mysterious seizures and dizzy spells. He would sometimes faint for no apparent reason. No one ever diagnosed his illness, but the symptoms

Eleanor did not have a close relationship with her mother, Anna Hall Roosevelt (above), who died when Eleanor was eight.

persisted for years. He became thin and weak, which frightened his family. His father thought that travel would be good for him. So Elliott spent several years away, first at boarding school, then on a ranch in Texas, and later on a tour to India.

By the time Elliott returned to New York, he was in his early twenties and more withdrawn, moody, and distracted than ever. While he had been gone, he had started drinking alcohol to lessen the effects of his illness. His drinking did not appear to be much of a concern. But unknown to his family, Elliott had become an alcoholic.

A BRILLIANT WEDDING

A few months after Elliott returned from India, he met Anna Hall and fell deeply in love. He described her as "womanly in all purity, holiness and beauty, an angel in tolerance, in forgiveness, and in faith."

Anna was fearful of Elliott's moodiness and sudden, violent outbursts. But he was handsome, charming, and completely devoted to her. So she agreed to marry him. In December 1883 the *New York Times* carried a story about the wedding, calling it "one of the most brilliant weddings of the season." Anna was nineteen years old, and Elliott was twenty-three.

ELEANOR ARRIVES IN A TROUBLED FAMILY

On October 11, 1884, Anna gave birth to Anna Eleanor Roosevelt, whom they called Eleanor. Elliott called Eleanor a miracle from heaven. He gave her a pet name, "little Nell." As for Anna, her increasing problems with Elliott made her cold and aloof. Anna was disappointed that her daughter wasn't beautiful. Anna gave the little girl a nickname, too: "Granny."

Eleanor tried very hard to win Anna's love. When Anna suffered from one of her headaches, Eleanor rubbed her temples. Eleanor realized that the way to be loved was to be useful.

Elliott spent most of his time traveling or hunting. He spent weekends in clubs where he drank for hours. Anna was miserable. To hide her unhappiness, she threw herself into the social scene, hosting lavish parties and attending high-society functions.

In the fall of 1889, Anna gave birth to the couple's second child, Elliott Roosevelt Jr. But Elliott Sr.'s drinking problem had grown more

Modern Marvels in Old New York

The New York City that Anna, Elliott, and Eleanor lived in was the largest, most modern city in the United States. Great structures were built during the 1880s that can still be seen in the city today:

- The Brooklyn Bridge. This suspension bridge is now dwarfed by steel and glass skyscrapers. But when it opened in 1883, it was the tallest structure in lower Manhattan—and the longest suspension bridge in the world.
- The Statue of Liberty. It is possible that Anna and Elliott could have taken Eleanor to the dedication of the statue in 1886. The statue was a gift from the French government to the people of the United States. It was built in France, disassembled, and shipped to America. Today, the statue still stands tall in New York harbor.

Eleanor had lost her mother; her father, Elliott Roosevelt (center); and one of her brothers, Elliott Roosevelt Jr. (right), before she turned ten.

severe. Finally, he and Anna agreed to take a trip to Europe with the family, in the hope that things could be repaired. The Roosevelts traveled for several months. While they were abroad, Anna gave birth to a boy named Gracie Hall.

But nothing helped Elliott's problems. Eventually he was confined to a mental hospital near Paris, France. Anna and the children returned home and faced the task of rebuilding their lives without him.

MORE TRAGEDIES FOR ELEANOR

Anna and Elliott agreed that he would remain away from the family for two years, until he could prove he was completely cured. He did manage to visit once in a while, and Eleanor lived for these rare visits.

On December 7, 1892, Anna died suddenly of diphtheria. She

was twenty-nine years old. Less than a year later, in May 1893, three-year-old Elliott Jr. died of scarlet fever and diphtheria. Eleanor's father was devastated. He began drinking again.

Elliott missed Eleanor terribly. However, Anna's mother Mary—known as Grandmother Hall—would not allow him to visit the children alone. So Elliott wrote Eleanor long, loving letters filled with descriptions of how they would be together. Eleanor read them over and over, clinging to the hope that she would one day live with him again.

It was not to be. On August 14, 1894, Elliott died. It is unclear what he died of, although it is thought that he succumbed to one of his mysterious seizures. Grandmother Hall wouldn't let Eleanor attend the funeral. Even in death, she was not allowed to see her beloved father.

After her mother died, Eleanor lived with her grandmother, who provided Eleanor the first stable and loving home she'd known.

Alone in a Big Family

By the time Eleanor was ten years old, her mother, father, and one brother were dead. After Elliott's death, it was decided that Eleanor and her brother Hall would remain with Grandmother Hall in her home near Tivoli, New York. Eleanor's four young aunts and uncles also lived there: Valentine (called Val), Edward, Edith, and Maude.

ELEANOR BEGINS TO HEAL

Slowly, Eleanor's life grew calmer. She had a stable, loving home. Her aunts and uncles taught her to ride horses, to play tennis, and to ride a bicycle. Eleanor later wrote that she marveled at her uncles and aunts, who always made her feel at home.

But life was not all freedom in Grandmother Hall's house. Grandmother made Eleanor wear ugly clothing and hot, scratchy wool stockings. She also made Eleanor walk for hours with a stick behind her

Eleanor was shy as a young girl and spent a lot of time alone riding horses and reading books.

shoulders to give her good posture, just as she had forced Eleanor's mother to do. Sundays were devoted to prayer, reading, and walks with her aunts and uncles.

Even though Grandmother Hall was strict, she loved Eleanor very much. The New York house was a place where Eleanor slowly began to heal from the wounds of her early childhood.

Eleanor attended a small school near her home. She learned to dance and play the piano. Eleanor spent endless hours reading in the branches of her favorite cherry tree. She began to write stories and poetry, much of it about nature. Eleanor began to realize how much beauty and knowledge was in the world, and she enjoyed learning.

ELEANOR'S FIRST ADVENTURE

When Eleanor was fifteen, Grandmother Hall called Eleanor into her room one day. She told Eleanor that her mother had always wanted her to go to boarding school abroad. So in the fall of 1899, Eleanor boarded a ship and sailed for England. She felt lost and lonely, with no idea what lay in store for her. Eleanor's destination was Allenswood, a small, respected girls' boarding school outside London. Wealthy families from around the world sent their daughters there.

ALLENSWOOD

Eleanor thrived at Allenswood. To her surprise and joy, Eleanor was popular. She made good grades in all her subjects, which included German, Latin, history, algebra, and literature. She took lessons on the piano and the violin. She discovered that she was quite athletic, and her six-foot height was an advantage in some sports. Even in her old age, she recalled the day she made the field hockey team and everyone cheered for her as the happiest day of her life. Eleanor became strong and confident.

The headmistress of Allenswood was a strong, fiery woman named Marie Souvestre. Eleanor was invited into Mlle Souvestre's circle of a few chosen students. (Mlle stands for "Mademoiselle," the French term for "Miss.") The group ate together and spent free time together, discussing events or reading aloud to one another. She encouraged Eleanor to discard her ugly, short dresses. So Eleanor began to dress in more attractive clothing.

During her three years at Allenswood, Eleanor excelled in academics and athletics, developing self-confidence and a sense of independence.

Marie Souvestre

Eleanor's teacher and mentor, Marie Souvestre, was one of the most influential people in Eleanor's life. Mlle Souvestre was born in France in 1830 and became a highly respected educator. She was a feminist, a humanitarian, and a natural leader who wanted her students to think for themselves and to explore the world. Passionate and opinionated, she encouraged all of her students to be the same. Eleanor's experiences at Allenswood under Mlle Souvestre's care deeply affected the young girl's outlook on life and on her own abilities. After Mlle Souvestre's death in 1905, Eleanor continued to display her picture on her desk.

Mlle Souvestre's encouragement gave Eleanor the freedom to express her emotions and the courage to satisfy her own wants and needs. This was astonishing to Eleanor, who had not been encouraged by her mother or her grandmother to have thoughts and feelings of her own.

ELEANOR SEES THE WORLD

During vacations, Eleanor traveled with friends. Several times, Mlle Souvestre invited Eleanor to travel with her. Eleanor later wrote that this was "one of the most momentous things that happened in my education." Mlle Souvestre gave Eleanor the responsibilities of planning the trips, packing, and making all the arrangements. Eleanor was surprised to find that she could do these things alone, and well.

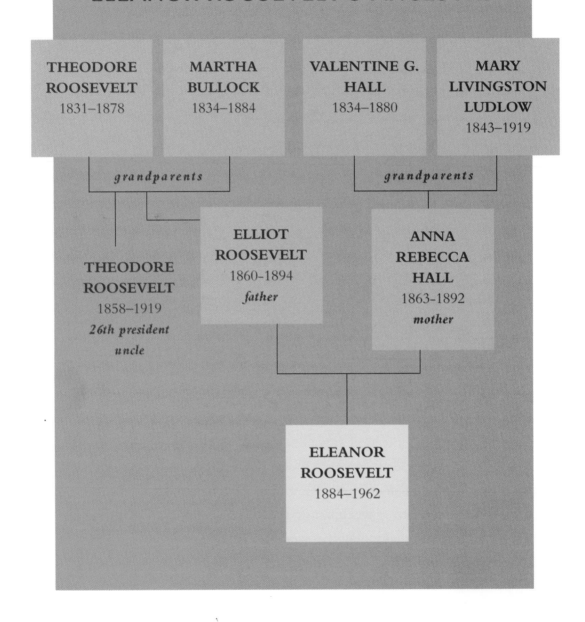

ELEANOR ROOSEVELT'S ANCESTRY

Mlle Souvestre encouraged Eleanor to eat native foods, drink local wines, and explore out-of-the-way places. Eleanor wrote, "Traveling with Mlle Souvestre was a revelation. She did all the things that in a vague way you had always felt you wanted to do."

A SAD GOODBYE

Eleanor spent three years at Allenswood. She grew from a sad, shy girl into a confident and strong young woman. Eleanor very much wanted to teach at Allenswood. She also thought that she might go on to college. But Grandmother Hall had other ideas.

Eleanor was, after all, a wealthy young society lady. She was expected to "come out" during her eighteenth year. That meant Eleanor would be a debutante, attending parties and dances to meet eligible young men. She dreaded the prospect, but Grandmother Hall's word was law.

Mlle Souvestre was afraid that Eleanor's hard-won confidence would be shattered. She urged Eleanor to save some of her energy for herself. But the glittering, chaotic world that Eleanor had left now pulled her back, and there was nothing that either of them could do about it.

Unlike the intellectual environment of Allenswood, life in New York for Eleanor (front row, second from right) was full of social obligations. Eleanor and her future husband Franklin (back row, third from right) often attended the same functions prior to their romance.

THREE

Coming Out and Growing Up

Because she was a Roosevelt, and because this was her coming-out year, Eleanor was automatically invited to the best parties. One of her first dances was agony for her. The custom was that each young lady carried a dance card, which young men would fill with their names. Then the lady would dance with each gentleman on her list during the evening. A lady's popularity was gauged by which young men signed her card and which dances they requested.

Eleanor was mortified to realize that her card was not full. The long stretches between dances were torture. She left early, deeply embarrassed

Franklin proposed to Eleanor while he was still a student at Harvard.

and ashamed that she was not the beautiful belle her mother had been. "By no stretch of the imagination," she wrote much later, "could I fool myself into thinking that I was a popular debutante."

But Eleanor was much more prepared for her role than she realized. She now wore expensive, flattering gowns for formal occasions. Her years at Allenswood had given her poise and confidence. Eleanor had an air of sophistication that the other debutantes lacked.

FRANKLIN

It was during this year that Eleanor was reacquainted with a distant cousin, Franklin Roosevelt. Franklin was a student at Harvard University, but he frequently visited New York. Since they were both part of high society, they met often at parties and dances.

Franklin and Eleanor made a striking couple on the dance floor. He was blond and attractive, charming and full of fun. He admired her beauty and her intelligence. Eleanor realized that he was gen-

Franklin's Early Years

Franklin Delano Roosevelt was born on January 30, 1882. His mother, Sara, spoiled him from the day he was born. She dressed him in elegant clothing and let his blond hair grow long, like a girl's. As he grew up, the other children thought him prissy and a "mama's boy." At school, he was not very good at sports, and he wasn't very well liked by the other students. By the time he reached Harvard University, he was an outsider in his set. Eventually, however, people came to like him better. He joined many clubs at college and worked on the school newspaper. By the time he met Eleanor, he was well liked, with many friends and a bright future.

uinely interested in her. Here was someone Eleanor could talk to, laugh with, and be serious with. He accepted her completely. Eleanor fell in love with the dashing Franklin, and he with her.

A FIRST GLIMPSE AT ANOTHER NEW YORK

Eleanor had made many friends by now. Several of them were interested in helping out the underprivileged people of New York City. They took her to visit the poorer sections of the city. Eleanor had never seen anything like it. The people lived in crowded, filthy tenement housing. They suffered from sickness, bad food, and terrible working conditions.

Eleanor visited settlement houses, which were places where poor people, usually immigrants, could learn English and take classes in a variety of subjects. Eleanor volunteered to teach calisthenics and fancy dancing to children at the College Settlement on New York City's Lower East Side. For the first time, she was face-to-face with the effects of poverty, and she was eager to do something to help.

Of course, Eleanor's family was shocked at the young woman's eagerness to spend time in the poorer areas of town. But Eleanor realized that she was doing valuable work—work that helped the lives of others. This gave her strength and confidence. It occurred to her that she might one day become a social worker or perhaps a teacher. She wanted to learn more.

ELEANOR CHOOSES ROMANCE

Eleanor worked at the settlement house during the day. Her evenings were filled with parties and the theater. And she had another, secret part of her life: her relationship with Franklin. Franklin was still at Harvard, but he had already proposed. She had accepted, knowing that she would have to give up her dream of working as a teacher or a social worker. But she was in love.

They kept their engagement secret for several months. Franklin was concerned that his mother, Sara, would not approve. Sure enough, when they did announce their engagement in the autumn of 1903, Sara was not happy. She insisted that they were too young to marry. Franklin would not be discouraged. Sara eventually came to accept the marriage.

A WEDDING TO REMEMBER

By 1905, Eleanor's Uncle Theodore, her father's older brother, had been elected to a second term as president of the United States. He agreed to give the bride away. But because he was president, the scheduling was problematic. Eleanor and Franklin agreed to be married in New York on March 17, St. Patrick's Day, because Uncle Theodore would already be in the city for a St. Patrick's Day parade.

That day, Theodore escorted a radiant Eleanor down the aisle. More than 200 guests admired Eleanor's heavy satin gown, with a frothy lace veil that her mother had worn at her wedding. Sara had given her a collar of pearls, which made Eleanor feel "decked out beyond description," she later wrote.

When the ceremony was over, the new couple prepared to receive congratulations from their guests, but Uncle Theodore immediately headed into the next room for refreshments—and everyone followed him! Eleanor and Franklin could do nothing but follow the crowd, which neither of them seemed to mind. Finally, they cut the cake, then left to change clothes. The guests showered them with rice as they climbed into a waiting carriage and began their married life.

Eleanor and Franklin married when she was twenty.

A Miserable Society Wife

After Franklin's studies at Harvard were over, the newlyweds set off on a proper three-month honeymoon in Europe.

The trip was wonderful for Eleanor. In London, they shopped for clothes, books, and other items. Franklin was an avid shopper, and he bought her many beautiful, expensive gifts.

There was only one dark spot that clouded their visit in London. In March, just a short time after the wedding, Mlle Souvestre had died. "Her death had been a great sorrow to me," Eleanor wrote, "coming as it did before I had an opportunity to visit Europe again."

The young couple moved on to Paris, where they ate at restaurants and spent their time shopping. Then it was on to Italy, where Eleanor was captivated by Milan, Venice, Florence, and Rome. In Venice, with its network of canals for streets, they rode a gondola over the waters and visited family friends. From Italy, they traveled to Germany, and then visited Scotland before returning home.

Eleanor gushed in her letters home that "I've never been so well looked after." But deep inside, she felt timid and unsure about Franklin and their relationship. His good looks attracted many women who would comment on how handsome and charming Franklin was. Eleanor began to worry about everything, including whether she would be able to please him. Franklin brushed off Eleanor's fears with a smile and a kiss, breezily telling her not to worry. For a time, that was enough, and Eleanor tried to relax.

SARA CONTROLS ELEANOR'S LIFE

The trip home on the ship was miserable for Eleanor. She was in her first months of pregnancy and was unwell for most of the crossing. When they arrived home, they discovered that Sara had rented a house for them. But Eleanor was upset to discover that Sara had also furnished it, decorated it, and hired all the servants to run it. Eleanor had been looking forward to having a house of her own for the first time in her life. Now she would feel like a visitor, just as she had when she lived with relatives as a child.

Sara's country home of Hyde Park was worse. Until their house in New York City was ready, the new couple stayed there. No one, not even

Franklin, made an effort to make Eleanor feel at home. In the cozy sitting room, there were two comfortable chairs—one for Sara and one for Franklin. Eleanor sat wherever she could find a place. Franklin didn't realize, or ignored, what was happening.

Eleanor thought the best way to please Sara was to be exactly what Sara wanted her to be. All of Eleanor's childhood insecurities came to the surface. The confidence she had felt at Allenswood melted away.

Franklin told her that any problems she had with his mother were hers to work out. His inability to listen to her or to take her feelings seriously made her feel betrayed and empty. Year after year, Eleanor grew more withdrawn.

On their honeymoon, Eleanor and Franklin visited many European cities, including Venice, Italy.

Hyde Park

Franklin's birthplace, Hyde Park, is located in New York State along the Hudson River. In the late 1800s, many wealthy families from New York City built enormous homes on vast estates in the area. Eleanor spent a great deal of time at Hyde Park during her marriage, and after Franklin's death, she gave it to the U.S. government for historic preservation. Today, Hyde Park is the location of the Franklin Delano Roosevelt Presidential Library and the Eleanor Roosevelt National Historic Site. Both Eleanor and Franklin are buried at Hyde Park.

UNPREPARED FOR MOTHERHOOD

Eleanor was also pregnant much of the time. She wrote that "for ten years I was always just getting over having a baby or about to have one." Anna Eleanor was born in 1906, James was born in 1907, and Franklin Jr. arrived in 1909. Franklin Jr. died a few months after he was born, and Eleanor gave birth to another son, Elliott, in 1910. She and Franklin would have two more sons, the second Franklin Jr. in 1914 and John in 1916. Eleanor had wanted to raise her children herself, but Sara insisted on hiring servants to care for them. Silently, Eleanor gave in again.

As the babies came and the children grew, Eleanor did find some pleasure in them and in her marriage. The family enjoyed summers at Campobello, another country house the family owned. It was on an island off the coast of Maine. Franklin and Eleanor spent time together, walking in the countryside or sailing in their small boat, the *Half Moon*. At

Campobello, Franklin and Eleanor had a measure of independence from Sara, and in many ways their marriage grew stronger.

But once the summers were over, they returned to life in New York. To pass her time, Eleanor went to the theater, took classes in languages, knitted, and embroidered. But these activities did not heal her feelings of sadness and discontent that grew with each passing year.

A NEW HOME—BUT STILL NOT HER OWN

In 1908, Sara had a house built for Franklin and Eleanor on East 65th Street in New York City. Sara also built another house for herself next door. Doors and passageways connected the two houses. Sara could come and go between them whenever she liked. Eleanor had little say in how the house was designed or furnished.

A few months after moving into the house, Eleanor was sitting at her dressing table when she began to cry. When Franklin appeared, Eleanor told him that she didn't like living in a house that was not hers. Rather than comforting his wife, he told her that he thought she was "quite mad" and that she would feel differently when she calmed down. Eleanor eventually dried her tears and went down to dinner.

Life had not turned out the way Eleanor had hoped. She thought she would find happiness with her husband and their family they would create together. Franklin loved her but he could not see that she needed someone to listen to her, to respect her thoughts, and to appreciate her ideas. Eleanor was completely miserable.

Eleanor and Franklin's political life began with his campaign for the New York Senate in 1910.

FIVE

Excitement of a Political Life

After Franklin had graduated from law school, he accepted a job with the respected law firm of Carter, Ledyard, and Milburn. Although he enjoyed being a lawyer, he had always wanted something more. In 1910, that something came knocking on the Roosevelts' door.

Several wealthy Democrats had been keeping their eye on the young Franklin. One day, the district attorney of Dutchess County, John Mack, visited Franklin to discuss his running for state senator. Franklin jumped at the chance to run for office. Sara was appalled at the idea of his running as a Democrat because many Roosevelts, including President Theodore, were Republicans. But Eleanor was delighted at the idea.

In October, only a week after Eleanor gave birth to their son Elliott, Franklin set off on his campaign tour. He gave speeches in tiny villages and larger towns. Even though he was a young unknown, he impressed everyone who met him. Franklin easily won the election.

POLITICAL AND INDEPENDENT

State senators usually lived in Albany, the state capital, so after Franklin's win, Eleanor and Franklin went to Albany and found a house. For the first time in her life, Eleanor finally had a home of her own.

Eleanor jumped eagerly into her responsibilities. One of the first things she did was to hire a completely new staff for the Albany house. Eleanor unpacked the family's belongings herself. She always had a passion for being completely settled as quickly as possible, wherever she lived. "I want all my photographs hung, all my ornaments out, and everything in order within the first twenty-four hours," she wrote.

The next day, Eleanor left to do her own shopping, taking the children along. She was shocked when a stranger approached her and said, "You must be Mrs. Roosevelt; your children are the only children I don't know!" The realization that everybody up and down the street would know what they were doing was a great surprise to Eleanor.

Another surprise to her was a new desire for independence that she felt stirring within her. "I had to stand on my own two feet now," she wrote, "and I think I knew that it was good for me. . . . I was beginning to realize that something within me craved to be an individual."

Within a few weeks she had made many friends. Her talent for putting others at ease, which she had showed as a young debutante, resurfaced. Eleanor genuinely cared about people's feelings and opinions, and people saw that. She became widely respected and admired.

Eleanor always claimed that she had no interest in politics. However, she threw herself into the political game with gusto. She spent hours at the capitol, listening to the senators as they debated. She began to form her own opinions about the senators and their positions. In some cases, she forged personal friendships with politicians who opposed Franklin and his political ideas.

Eleanor's newfound independence gave her a renewed sense of confidence. She became closer with her children. Eleanor made many changes in the way she dealt with her children. No matter how many meetings or errands she had to run, she was home each afternoon to be with them. They had tea together; then she played games with or read to them.

Another bright spot in Eleanor's life was her younger brother, Hall. In 1912, Hall was twenty years old and a senior in college. "I loved him deeply

Initially, Eleanor felt unprepared for motherhood but soon took pleasure in her children, reading to and playing games with them.

and longed to mean a great deal in his life," Eleanor wrote. He decided to marry a lovely young woman named Margaret Richardson, and Eleanor approved. It was a happy time for everyone.

THE ROOSEVELTS GO TO WASHINGTON

In 1912, Woodrow Wilson was elected president of the United States, and Franklin was reelected to the state senate. In April 1913, Wilson called Franklin to Washington and appointed him assistant secretary of the Navy.

Eleanor was anxious. She had become accustomed to the role of a state senator's wife, but now she would be the wife of a high-ranking U.S. administration official. After spending the summer with the children at Campobello, Eleanor left for Washington with her family.

Franklin's political work required much travel, and Eleanor sometimes accompanied him on trips.

Life in Washington was as chaotic and hectic as Eleanor thought it would be. She took it upon herself to visit the young wives of Navy officers, offering friendship and comfort. Her experience in Albany had been a good lesson in how to deal with new people. "I must have come a long way since I moved up to Albany," she wrote, "for then I never could have paid those first calls."

Her relationship with Franklin had come a long way, too. By 1913, their marriage was as strong as it had ever been. Now Eleanor relied on her own skills and intelligence to get things done. Franklin responded to this with a newfound warmth. They had developed a partnership based on shared beliefs and a deep affection for one another.

But there was still some tension between them. Franklin loved parties and drinking. Eleanor, who had lived with alcoholics, could not stand to be around people who lost control of themselves. She tried to share in the fun, but it was hard for her. Eleanor encouraged him to go out with his friends alone, which he did. They began to have different groups of friends. However, they still attended endless dinners and parties together, and they entertained in their own home regularly. Eleanor and Franklin became one of the most well-respected and popular couples in Washington.

WORLD WAR I

Europe erupted into war in August 1914, and although the United States was not fighting, it tore the country apart all the same. People in favor of the war argued with those against it. Some wanted the United States to enter the war, while many others insisted that the country stay

The War to End All Wars

World War I was known as "The Great War" and "The War to End All Wars" when it was fought in the early years of the twentieth century.

There had been much unrest in Europe in the years before World War I began. Tensions among people of different countries and different ethnic backgrounds ran high. European nations began raising large armies and passing laws to protect their own interests. They also began forming alliances and agreed to protect one another if any kind of conflict should occur.

The war started as a local clash between two countries, Austria-Hungary and Serbia. On June 28, 1914, Archduke Francis Ferdinand of Austria-Hungary was assassinated by a Serbian nationalist. The two countries declared war on each other. The allies of each country quickly joined the fight. It eventually turned into a global war that involved thirty-two countries. The United States entered the conflict in 1917 when it declared war on Germany.

World War I is considered to be the first modern war. Modern inventions such as airplanes and tanks were used in warfare for the first time. It was also the most deadly war ever fought up to that time. Though exact numbers are hard to establish, tens of millions of people were left dead, wounded, or missing in World War I. And millions of those deaths were due to disease that spread among soldiers and local populations. Most people hoped that World War I would be the last war ever fought. Sadly, however, the destruction the war caused, combined with the political compromises forced on countries such as Germany, laid the foundation for World War II, which would erupt twenty-one years later.

out of it. Franklin was convinced that the Navy had to prepare for war just in case, but few others in the government listened to him. Eleanor was sympathetic to Franklin's position and urged him to follow his convictions. Then in 1917, the United States entered the war.

The war changed Eleanor's life in Washington. She threw herself into the war effort—visiting Navy hospitals, volunteering with the Red Cross, and working with groups that knitted clothing and distributed small personal items to soldiers.

With Eleanor's newfound work, and Franklin's preoccupation with his job, the two began to see less of each other. Franklin spent weeks out of town. When he was home, he stayed out late. He began spending time with people whom Eleanor did not care for. She made no secret of the fact that most of the parties bored her. By 1917, Franklin was spending very little time with Eleanor and the children.

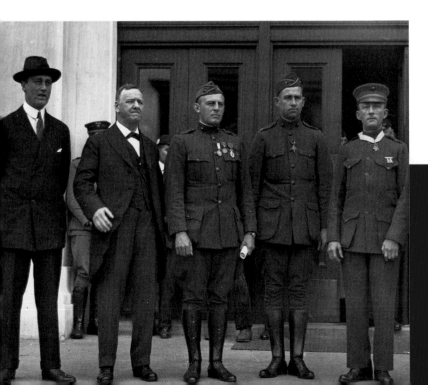

While Franklin (left) was the assistant secretary of the Navy, the United States entered World War I.

Lucy Mercer

The woman who almost ended Eleanor's marriage was the young, beautiful daughter of a well-respected, but impoverished, Washington family. Because her family had lost its fortune, Lucy was forced to earn a living. She became Eleanor's social secretary in 1914. It is unclear when Lucy and Franklin began their affair. But there were many times when Franklin and Lucy were seen together in public when Eleanor was out of town. Most of their friends knew about the affair, but they kept the secret from Eleanor.

In 1920, Lucy married a wealthy widower named Winthrop Rutherford. But the relationship between Franklin and Lucy never really ended. Although he had promised Eleanor he would never see Lucy again, he broke that promise. For instance, he arranged for a limousine to take Lucy to his inauguration, and she attended several parties and functions at the White House during his presidency.

"THE BOTTOM DROPPED OUT OF MY WORLD"

In the fall of 1918, Eleanor was visiting Sara at Hyde Park when she received a telegram. Franklin had been on a trip, and he had become ill. They met him in New York City and took him back to Hyde Park. As Eleanor was unpacking his things, she found a small packet of letters. They were love letters to Franklin from Lucy Mercer, Eleanor's secretary.

Eleanor was devastated. She confronted him with the evidence and offered him a divorce. Sara threatened to cut Franklin off from the family fortune if he left Eleanor for Lucy. Franklin knew that his political career would be over if he was divorced. Eleanor and Franklin finally reached an agreement. She would stay in the marriage if he promised never to see Lucy Mercer again. Franklin agreed.

Eleanor's world was broken. But she decided to keep trying, no matter how much Franklin had hurt her. She did still love him, after all, and he said he still loved her. Franklin began paying more attention to Eleanor and the family. He bought her gifts and invited her on official Navy trips. Eleanor tried harder to share Franklin's enjoyment of parties and nightlife. Slowly they began to rebuild their marriage. But their relationship was never the same again.

Franklin's affair with Eleanor's social secretary, Lucy Mercer Rutherford, nearly ended the Roosevelts' marriage.

Family was important to Eleanor (standing), but the death of Grandmother Hall (left) made her realize that she needed to devote herself to her children as well as to worthy causes.

SIX

Eleanor Finds Her Voice

In 1918, World War I ended, and people in the United States rejoiced. But for Eleanor, the postwar period was a time of sadness and uncertainty. She had no idea how she would rebuild her trust and confidence in Franklin, and in herself. In 1919, sorrow touched her life in another way when Grandmother Hall died. "Her life was a sad one in many ways," Eleanor wrote. "Yet those who were close to her mourned her deeply."

Grandmother Hall's death made Eleanor think about the importance of having one's own life. If Grandmother Hall had not given up her own life for her children, would they all have been better off? Eleanor made a promise to herself: she would never be dependent on her children by allowing all her interests to center on them as her grandmother had done.

ELEANOR ON THE CAMPAIGN TRAIL

The year 1920 was a presidential election year, and it was also the year Congress passed the Nineteenth Amendment to the U.S. Constitution, giving women the right to vote. Eleanor was elated at the passage of the amendment, but she was less thrilled with the fact that, at the Democratic National Convention that summer, Franklin was nominated for vice president. The highlight of the campaign season was a four-week train trip from New York to Colorado. Eleanor was the only woman on the train. She had nothing to do but knit, read, write letters, and look at the scenery speeding by. Franklin never asked for her ideas or opinions, and she was virtually ignored by everyone onboard. When the train stopped and Franklin gave a speech, she had to stand by, smiling and waving at the crowd.

The only person who noticed Eleanor's unhappiness was one of Franklin's political friends, Louis Howe. Louis began to come to her

In 1920, Roosevelt ran unsuccessfully for vice president of the United States.

room to ask her advice. He gave her drafts of speeches to look over and asked her opinion about press conferences.

Eleanor was appalled by Louis's appearance. "He . . . gave the impression that at times cleanliness was not of particular interest to him," she wrote. But his honest desire to hear her thoughts won her over. Louis began to teach her about the workings of politics. This was the beginning of a close friendship between Eleanor and Louis. He saw in Eleanor a strength of character that others, even Franklin, missed.

The Democrats lost badly in the election. The Roosevelts returned to New York City, where Franklin went back to his work as a lawyer. As for Eleanor, she began to build a new life.

NEW FRIENDS, NEW CHALLENGES

A few days after she arrived in New York, Eleanor was invited to be a part of a political organization called the New York State League of Women Voters. They strongly believed in such things as health insurance, a minimum-wage law, and an end to child labor.

It was through her work with the league that she began to meet strong, interesting women who would become close friends. One was Esther Lape, a teacher and a journalist. Esther's life partner, Elizabeth Read, was a graduate of Smith College and one of the first female lawyers in the United States. They ate fabulous meals together, read to one another, and endlessly discussed politics. These women genuinely cared about Eleanor as a person. Her emotional well-being and her feelings were important to them. After only a few weeks with her new friends, Eleanor was reborn. The world seemed rich with possibilities.

Polio

The disease that crippled Franklin was polio, which is short for poliomyelitis. Symptoms of polio include headache, fever, sore throat, and stiffness. Some cases of polio are mild. Severe cases can cause crippling, paralysis, and sometimes death. The polio virus is spread through infected fecal matter.

The disease had been known long before Franklin caught it. It usually struck small children, and Franklin's case was somewhat rare. Later, by the 1950s, tens of thousands of people had been infected with polio.

In 1952, a research scientist at the University of Pittsburgh, Dr. Jonas Salk, discovered a successful polio vaccine. When tests of the vaccine began in 1954, new cases of polio fell dramatically. Today, the World Health Organization (WHO) is working to eliminate polio completely from the world.

A NEW AND UNEXPECTED BATTLE

In August 1921, the family went to Campobello as usual. Franklin and the children sailed, swam, fished, and played together. But he began to complain of feeling tired, which was unlike him. On August 10, Franklin once again complained of feeling tired. He thought a vigorous swim would do him good, so he and the children headed for the lake. Afterward, Franklin sat on the porch in his wet bathing suit, reading his mail. Soon he began to feel a chill and went up to bed.

The next day, Franklin had a high fever. Over the next few days, he began to have terrible pains in his back and legs. No one knew what was wrong. For three weeks, Franklin lay sick in bed, sometimes unable to move or to feel his arms and legs at all. Finally, his condition was diagnosed. He had polio. His legs were paralyzed. He would never walk unaided again. Franklin was quietly transported back to their New York home.

Sara insisted that Franklin accept his disability. Eleanor insisted that he would regain his strength and resume his political career. The two women battled daily. But Eleanor would not back down this time. Slowly, Sara began to realize that she would not get her way.

Franklin's illness changed his relationship with Eleanor. His affair had destroyed any hope of romantic love between them. What replaced that love was a sense of mutual respect, admiration, and understanding. In many ways, Franklin's illness strengthened their marriage. They forged a new partnership that they would come to rely on for the rest of their lives.

Franklin was diagnosed with polio in 1921, and though the condition was debilitating, he did all he could, including exercising and spending time in a warm climate, to regain his strength.

Driving a car was one of many skills Eleanor learned as a result of Franklin's illness.

SEVEN

A Life of Her Own

Franklin's illness changed Eleanor's outlook on life completely. Her new appreciation for him, along with his admiration for her, gave her renewed strength. It also made Eleanor aware that she would now have to be both father and mother to her children. The two younger boys, Franklin Jr. and John, were accustomed to hard play and a lot of activity. Eleanor realized she would have to become a more well-rounded person than she had ever been before. She took swimming lessons and began driving her own car. She learned to enjoy hiking, camping, and other outdoor activities. Her determination to become "more companionable" gave her energy and a sense of satisfaction.

Eleanor found political work, such as participating in a women's advisory committee, fulfilling.

BOLD STEPS INTO A NEW WORLD

Franklin was determined not to be inactive for the rest of his life. He began traveling to Florida, where he could swim and exercise his legs in a warmer climate. Eventually, Franklin purchased a run-down resort in Georgia called Warm Springs. He spent much of the 1920s at Warm Springs, working to regain as much strength as possible.

Eleanor preferred to stay in New York and pursue the new independent life she had begun before his illness. Again, the two of them created separate lives, with separate sets of friends and interests. This unique arrangement suited them both perfectly.

Less than a year after Franklin's illness set in, Eleanor joined a political group called the Women's Division of the Democratic State Committee. Louis Howe encouraged her. He felt that it would be a good way for the Roosevelt name to stay in politics. But Eleanor had become very interested in the political world in her own right, and she had begun to realize that she had something to contribute.

It was through this political work that Eleanor met two women who would become her closest friends for the next fifteen years, Nancy Cook and Marion Dickerman. Cook, a college graduate and excellent political organizer, worked with the Democratic State Committee. She and Eleanor became friends from the moment they met at a luncheon. Dickerman, a politician and educator, was Nancy's partner. Eleanor spent time with them in their Greenwich Village apartment, and the three women often traveled together. When Eleanor was with them, she had fun. When they were apart, Eleanor wrote long letters, telling them how much she missed them.

Eleanor became involved in many activities. She and some other women began a small newspaper for the Democratic State Committee. In 1922, she gave her first political speech. Before long, she became a popular speaker at luncheons and events throughout the state.

The Women's Trade Union League (WTUL)

This powerful group was founded in 1903 as the first national organization devoted to women workers. The league's goal was to unite women from all classes to work together to improve working conditions. By 1904, the WTUL had branches in New York, Chicago, and Boston. From 1907 until 1922, the year Eleanor joined, the organization fought for several reforms, such as an eight-hour workday, a minimum-wage law, the end of night work for women, and the abolition of child labor. Members of the WTUL also joined strikes, or refusals to work, by female workers in the garment industry in order to obtain better working conditions.

By the 1920s, the influence of the WTUL began to fade. It faced financial problems during the 1930s and 1940s, and it was dissolved in 1950.

Another political organization Eleanor joined was the Women's Trade Union League. Through this group, Eleanor was exposed to the lives of poorer working women. She was aware that her privileged background gave her no sense of how ordinary people lived. She began to believe that every person deserved a job that paid enough not only to cover living expenses, but also to enjoy small luxuries, to provide for their health, and to make sure their children could get an education.

She also began to think about the role of women in society. During this time, most women were expected to stay home with their children. Working women were looked upon with suspicion. It was thought that a woman could not be a mother and have a career at the same time.

During the 1920s, Eleanor began to see that this was not the case. The vote gave women a voice in politics for the first time. Women could, and should, she believed, have a life outside their homes, whether they chose motherhood or not. Her own growth from a miserable, timid society matron to a happy, strong political leader was a good example of this.

Eleanor had begun surrounding herself with women who were capable of being active in politics and of having rich, fulfilling lives. To Eleanor, this was a revelation. It was during these years that she began to form opinions about the equality of women and of minorities that she would hold for the rest of her life.

VAL-KILL

Franklin encouraged Eleanor's friendships with Nancy, Marion, and the other women in her life. They gave her a closeness and intimacy that the couple's marriage lacked. He knew that he had been insensitive to her

The Eleanor Roosevelt National Historic Site

Eleanor once said, "The greatest thing I have learned is how good it is to come home again." Val-Kill was the only real home that Eleanor ever considered to be her own, and she cherished it all her life. During her lifetime, Val-Kill was her refuge from the world and her private sanctuary where she lived with her friends Nancy Cook and Marion Dickerman.

When Eleanor died in 1962, the house was turned into four apartments. In 1970, the land was sold to developers. A group of concerned citizens banded together to save Eleanor's house from destruction. This began a drive to turn the area into a national memorial.

The Eleanor Roosevelt National Historic Site was created in 1977 by President Jimmy Carter. Today, Val-Kill has been restored, and visitors from around the world can see the beautiful gardens and simple cottage that Eleanor called home.

needs and had hurt her deeply. Now he saw how much her new life meant to her, and he welcomed it wholeheartedly.

One late-summer day, Franklin, Eleanor, and some of her friends were picnicking near Hyde Park. Eleanor commented that it would be the last outing of the year, since Sara was closing the house for the winter. Franklin told her she was silly, because he owned the land. He encouraged Eleanor and her friends to build a cottage of their own in the nearby countryside.

Eleanor, Marion, and Nancy were thrilled with the idea. Franklin had a lovely stone cottage with a swimming pool built for them near the spot. By April 1926, the cottage was finished. They called it Val-Kill, after the small stream that flowed nearby. It became the women's hideaway, and they treasured it. They had linens and towels made for Val-Kill, monogrammed with their three initials: E.M.N. They received house-warming gifts from Franklin and their friends. Franklin jokingly referred to Val-Kill as the Honeymoon Cottage. Later Eleanor, Nancy, and Marion added a furniture workshop to the property and employed several local people in the manufacture of fine furniture.

Val-Kill—along with Nancy and Marion—became the center of Eleanor's life. The women traveled together, took Eleanor's boys camping, and worked together in politics. When they were at Val-Kill, they

Eleanor (second from right) received much comfort, support, and affection from her close female friends Nancy (second from left) and Marion (right), who shared her interests in politics and women's rights.

shared the most satisfying and private times with one another. Marion and Nancy gave Eleanor the affection, respect, and attention that she had always needed. They loved each other deeply.

ELEANOR BECOMES A TEACHER

Marion Dickerman was the vice principal at the Todhunter School, a private girls' school in New York. In 1926, she told Eleanor that the school's owner was going to sell the school. Eleanor suggested that Marion, Nancy, and she buy the school. They did, and Eleanor began her career as a teacher.

Eleanor taught American history, American literature, English, and current events. In every class, she tried to teach her students to think for themselves, as Mlle Souvestre had taught her. Most of her students were the daughters of wealthy New York families, just as she had been. Eleanor made it a point to take the girls on field trips to the poorer sections of town. She wanted them to understand the problems of poverty and the ways that the government could help.

A POLITICAL FORCE IN HER OWN RIGHT

Throughout the 1920s, Eleanor threw herself into political work. She participated in demonstrations, supported laws against child labor, and helped to raise funds for health clinics for mothers and children. Eleanor gave radio addresses on many topics related to women. She had a reputation for speaking candidly about almost any subject. Her public appearances became national news. Newspapers such as the *New York Times* wrote articles about Eleanor. She had become one of the best-known Democrats in the country.

Eleanor remained active in causes that concerned her while still fulfilling her obligations as a politician's wife.

A Political Wife Again— on Her Own Terms

The year 1928 was a watershed year for Eleanor. She had become a respected and popular voice in the Democratic Party. She wrote magazine articles, gave speeches and radio addresses, and traveled.

Franklin's years at Warm Springs had strengthened his arms and upper body, although his legs would always be paralyzed. He could walk short distances with a cane and heavy leg braces, while someone supported him. He decided it was time to return to politics. When the Democratic Party

As Eleanor matured, she understood how important it was for her to balance her interests with her responsibilities as a politician's wife, such as hosting social functions.

asked him to run for governor of New York in 1928, he agreed. To Eleanor's great surprise, Franklin won the election.

ELEANOR BREAKS THE RULES

Eleanor was forty-four years old when Franklin became governor of New York. Eleanor was delighted that her husband had won. But she feared that she would have to stop her own work, which she loved. Finally, she decided that she would not give up her hard-won new life. Eleanor was going to change the rules.

Eleanor created a schedule that would allow her to live the traditional role of governor's wife while continuing her work. On Sunday nights, Eleanor took the train from Albany to New York City. She taught at the Todhunter School from Mondays through Wednesdays. On Wednesday afternoons she returned to Albany, where she hosted teas, gave and attended dinners, and participated in all the social functions expected of a governor's wife. In between all these activities, she wrote letters and magazine articles, gave interviews and speeches, and did as much as

A Guard for "The Lady"

Eleanor wanted to be free to come and go as she pleased. But Franklin insisted that she have a bodyguard, and Earl Miller was assigned this job.

Miller, a former state trooper and military officer, was tall, athletic, and good looking. He had once been a circus acrobat, a swimmer, and a member of the U.S. Olympic boxing team. He and Eleanor became good friends immediately.

Earl accompanied Eleanor wherever she went, such as when she inspected hospitals and prisons as New York's first lady. He also went with her to Val-Kill, Hyde Park, and Campobello. He gave her a mare named Dot that Eleanor rode every day. He also gave Eleanor a nickname, "The Lady."

she could with the other organizations she belonged to. No other governor's wife had ever been so busy outside the governor's mansion.

EYES AND EARS OF THE GOVERNOR

Because Franklin was disabled, he could not travel easily. He began to send Eleanor everywhere, to be his "eyes and ears" among the people of New York State. She reported what she saw and heard, along with her own ideas of the problems New Yorkers faced.

Eleanor learned how to observe, and what details to look for, when she first began these inspections. "I learned to look in the cooking pots on the stove to find out if the contents corresponded to the menu," she later wrote. "I learned to notice whether the beds were too close together, and whether they were folded up and put in closets or behind doors during the day, which would indicate that they filled the corridors at night."

THE CRASH OF 1929

In October 1929, the stock market had crashed. Overnight, millions of people lost everything. Thousands of homeless and jobless men wandered the streets. Eleanor kept sandwiches and coffee available at her New York house for anyone who needed a meal.

For the next three years, the situation grew worse. By the presidential election of 1932, the American people desperately needed a new president who would bring them hope.

ON TO THE WHITE HOUSE

"Franklin did not tell me when he decided to run for the Presidency," Eleanor wrote in her autobiography. But it was no surprise to her that he decided to run. She didn't want Franklin to be president. She was convinced that she would have to give up everything

Eleanor cherished her independence and initially thought Franklin's run for president in 1932 would jeopardize it.

Black Thursday

The 1920s were a time of great prosperity for the United States. Ordinary Americans began investing in the stock market. Some people invested their life savings on the gamble of becoming rich.

On Thursday, October 24, 1929, stock prices began to fall. People panicked and began selling their stocks on the New York Stock Exchange. By the end of the day, prices on the stock market had fallen an average of 9 percent. Businesses and individuals who owned stocks lost millions of dollars. Gradually businesses failed, banks closed, and people lost everything they had. Many people committed suicide rather than face this disaster.

to be a silent White House hostess. Throughout the campaign of 1932, she was depressed and distracted.

During the campaign, Franklin and Eleanor were hounded by the press. One reporter who covered them was a woman named Lorena Hickok. Hickok was one of the few female reporters in the country. Hickok followed Eleanor as she visited towns, tramped through cornfields, and ate barbeque at an Arizona ranch. As the campaign wore on, the two became friends.

Eleanor told Hickok about her unhappy childhood and about her fears for her own lifestyle if Franklin won the presidency. Hickok told about her abusive family and the loss of her own mother when she was thirteen. Their friendship grew stronger. Eventually, Eleanor began calling her Hick, and the nickname stuck. Eleanor asked Hick's advice and respected her political opinions.

Lorena Alice Hickok

The woman who would become Eleanor's closest friend and confidant was born in Wisconsin in 1893. Lorena's father, Addison, regularly abused her. She ran away from home when she was fourteen and found work as a maid. For two years, she bounced from job to job and family to family, until her mother's cousin Ella Ellis took her in for good.

Lorena enrolled in college, but she soon left to become a reporter. At the time, it was thought that women could only cover "soft" news, such as parties and charity events. But Lorena convinced her editor to move her to the city desk. There she became known as a talented interviewer.

Lorena met Eleanor in 1932. After working with New Deal organizations in the 1930s, "Hick" moved into the White House to be with Eleanor in 1940. After Franklin's death, Hick and Eleanor continued to maintain their close friendship. They worked together on a book, *Women of Courage*, and Hick wrote a biography of Eleanor called *Reluctant First Lady*. Hick died in 1968.

"I WAS DEEPLY TROUBLED"

Franklin won the presidential election of 1932. Eleanor was forty-eight years old when she became first lady of the United States. "I was deeply troubled," she wrote. "As I saw it, this meant the end of any personal life of my own."

Eleanor had no idea what kind of role she would play as first lady. All she knew was that she did not want the life of a dutiful political wife. "Now," she wrote, "I shall have to work out my own salvation."

Eleanor set a new precedent in the White House, altering assumptions about the first lady's role.

NINE

"Eleanor Everywhere"

In the weeks between the election and the inauguration, Eleanor's most immediate problem was coordinating the move out of the governor's mansion in Albany and into the White House. In Washington, D.C., she met with Mrs. Herbert Hoover, the current president's wife, and the White House staff. Finally, all the arrangements were made, and there was nothing left to do but begin her life as first lady.

But Eleanor was not idle during this time. Even before the inauguration, she began writing two books. One was about her father, Elliott Roosevelt. *Hunting Big Game in the Eighties: The Letters of Elliott Roosevelt* detailed Elliott's adventures and travels when he was a young man.

The second book was titled *It's Up to the Women*. Eleanor firmly believed that women had the strength and the power to do great things,

Even at the White House, Eleanor was insistent on doing things her way, not necessarily the way they'd always been.

and that it was up to them to control their lives. In this book, she put forth many of her ideas about women and their role in society. She urged women to support changes that would help them and their families. It was an important book, written at a time when women still faced a great deal of discrimination. Millions around the country were inspired by her book when it was published in 1933.

A FRIGHTENED AND UNSURE COUNTRY

By 1932, the Great Depression had deepened. People who had once been wealthy were now selling apples or pencils on street corners. People were so frightened of bank closings that if their bank was still open, they withdrew all their money and hid it in their homes. Hungry families lined up for blocks at makeshift soup kitchens.

Franklin had run his campaign on the promise that he could help fix the country's problems. The previous sum-

Eleanor's Thoughts on Women and Jobs

Eleanor's book *It's Up to the Women* caused a great deal of controversy when it was published. The chapter that upset people the most was entitled "Women and Jobs." Eleanor stressed that it was vital that women work outside the home for their own happiness, regardless of whether they were single or married. Women could not achieve economic or personal independence without meaningful work. She did not see why there should be a conflict between a career and home. Eleanor wrote, "A woman, just like a man, may have a great gift for some particular thing. That does not mean that she must give up the joy of marrying and having a home and children."

mer, in his acceptance speech for the Democratic nomination, he had said, "I pledge you, I pledge myself, to a new deal for the American people." Franklin believed that it was the government's job to help Americans combat the effects of the Depression. His bold ideas would be known as the New Deal.

By the time of the inauguration, Eleanor had regained some of her confidence and courage. The morning before the inauguration, Eleanor and Hick sneaked out of downtown Washington and went to Rock Creek Cemetery. Eleanor wanted to take Hick to see the statue that had given Eleanor so much comfort in her earlier days. As they sat in the quiet cemetery, Eleanor told Hick how she used to come to the statue alone when she felt troubled or unhappy.

The next day, Eleanor stood beside Franklin as he recited the oath of office for the presidency. She felt proud of Franklin as he gave a stirring, courageous speech to the assembled crowd. "This great Nation will endure as it has endured . . . let me assert my firm belief that the only thing we have to fear is fear itself—nameless, unreasoning, unjustified terror."

A NEW LIFE, AGAIN

As soon as Eleanor settled into the White House, she began a major overhaul of the mansion and the way it was run. Eleanor disliked the stiff, formal rules of the White House, such as having guests ushered in by the staff. Instead, Eleanor met her own personal guests at the door whenever she could.

She shocked most of the longtime staff with her bold, new actions. She wrote that "my first act was to insist on running the elevator myself without waiting for one of the doormen to run it for me." When the chief usher complained that manning the elevator wasn't done by a president's wife, Eleanor got into the elevator, shut the door, and said, "Now it is!"

POWER OF THE PRESS

Most first ladies had stayed away from the press. Some had never even granted an interview. But Eleanor would be different, of course. She and Hick devised a plan. Eleanor would have regular press conferences, but only women reporters would be allowed in. National newspapers that did not have women on staff scrambled to hire women to cover Eleanor. These women knew they had Eleanor to thank for their jobs, and they became very protective of the first lady.

Eventually, Eleanor became even more involved in the American press. In 1934, she started broadcasting a weekly radio show. She continued to write articles for publications such as *Redbook*, *The Woman's Democratic News*, and the *Woman's Home Companion*. In 1935, at Hick's suggestion, Eleanor also began a daily syndicated newspaper column called "My Day." It began as a chatty look into the life of the first lady, but it became a forum for Eleanor to talk about issues and ideas that were important to her.

"My Day"

Six days a week, from 1935 until 1962, Eleanor wrote a syndicated newspaper column called "My Day." The only time she missed writing it was when Franklin died in 1945, and then she missed only four days. She wrote about political issues, current events, and private moments in her life. Here are some quotations from her column:

- On campaigning with Franklin: "My husband insisted always that a man stood on his own record. . . . I think he sometimes found it amusing to let me do things just so as to find out what the reaction of the public would be. But nothing we did was ever calculated and thought out as part of the campaign."
- On watching television: "If the use of leisure time is confined to looking at TV for a few extra hours every day, we will deteriorate as a people."
- On leaving the White House: "Now, I have spent my last night in the White House. I have had my last breakfast on the sun porch. And all today, I shall be saying goodbye to different people who have been loyal and kind. . . . Yet I cannot feel that it is goodbye for, when you are fond of people, you are sure to meet again."

As Eleanor settled into her new life, she found more and more things to occupy her time and energy. She was invited to speak at hundreds of luncheons, dinners, and meetings all over the country. She toured parks, prisons, hospitals, mines, and schools. She met with the leaders of various organizations and political groups to listen to their concerns and try to help them solve problems.

The reporters assigned to cover her were astounded at the energy she had. A typical day for Eleanor might begin with a meeting with an official or the leader of some group, followed by a luncheon where she might give a speech. In the afternoon, she would meet with foreign dignitaries, travel to yet another speech, and then return to the White House for a state dinner or other official function. After that, she would retire to her rooms, where she would write letters and plan the next day's activities. Eleanor was so busy, it seemed impossible that one person could be in all those places at one time. She got the nickname "Eleanor Everywhere."

As first lady, Eleanor attended so many functions that her nickname was "Eleanor Everywhere."

"The Worst Place I'd Ever Seen"

Hick reported on the conditions she found at a town called Morgantown, in the Scott's Run area of West Virginia. "Morgantown was the worst place I'd ever seen," she wrote. "In a gutter, along the main street through the town, there was stagnant, filthy water, which the inhabitants used for drinking, cooking, washing, and everything else imaginable. On either side of the street were ramshackle houses, black with coal dust, which most Americans would not have considered fit for pigs."

Eleanor also found a way to affect national politics directly. In the past, most first ladies were not involved with the president and his job. Eleanor set out to change that, too. Beside Franklin's bed was a basket. Each night, Eleanor wrote memos about pressing issues she felt Franklin should address and put the memos in the basket. The ideas in "Eleanor's basket" were among the first things Franklin read each day. In this way, Eleanor was able to influence a great deal of government policy.

ARTHURDALE

Hick and Eleanor had become closer than ever in the months after the inauguration. Eleanor relied on her for emotional support and comfort, and Hick was more than glad to be there for her friend. But Hick's job as a reporter began to suffer because of her intimacy with the first lady. Hick realized that her love for Eleanor made it very difficult for her to write about Eleanor fairly. So in 1933, Hick joined the staff of the Federal

Emergency Relief Administration. This government department was created by Franklin in the first few months of his presidency to give assistance to the nation's poor. Hick's job was to travel around the country and report on the success of the department's programs.

One of the poorest areas Hick visited was the Scott's Run area of West Virginia. When Hick saw it for the first time, she was horrified. Unemployed miners and their families lived in shacks. The people slept on dirty, insect-filled blankets. All of them were hungry. Many of the children did not go to school every day because they had to take turns using the only good dress or pair of shoes the family owned.

Eleanor arranged to visit herself. She was as appalled as Hick had been. This visit galvanized Eleanor's belief that workers in America deserved better treatment.

Eleanor imagined building a clean, tidy community of comfortable houses. Each family could grow their own food. Business or industry in the area would provide stable jobs at a living wage. There would be crafts, music, concerts, and other pastimes for the people to enjoy.

Arthurdale Today

Most of the original houses in Arthurdale are still standing. Many residents are descendants of the original Arthurdale settlers, and they are very proud of their past. The town of Arthurdale includes a 1,102-acre (446-hectare) historic district and the New Deal Homestead Museum. The town's Wagner Homestead is a fully restored 1930s working farm.

Children would have a local school, and no one would be left out because they had no good clothes or shoes. When Eleanor told Franklin about her idea, he supported it.

Eleanor held a press conference in November 1933 to discuss the idea, which was now called Arthurdale. The project was named for Richard Arthur, the man who sold the government his land for the project. By Thanksgiving, the land had been cleared and plowed, and by December, many of the houses were being built.

Immediately, there were huge problems with the construction, and costs soared. The project was ridiculed by the press and by people opposed to it. People were shocked that houses with indoor plumbing—an expensive luxury in those days—would be given to poor, dirty people.

Finally, after months of delay and mountains of criticism, the first fifty Arthurdale houses were completed and the families moved in. The

Though many criticized Eleanor's Arthurdale project as expensive and unsuccessful, Eleanor was proud to have helped house and care for hardworking Americans.

plan was that the families would remain on public welfare until they could plant crops and get decent jobs. At first, this plan seemed good. But problems arose again. No company wanted to build a factory in Arthurdale. Residents discovered that they couldn't grow enough food to feed their families. It took years for the people to find work and become self-sufficient.

Arthurdale drew a great deal of media attention—and scorn. Newspapers scoffed at the community and the costs of building it. People in the government considered Arthurdale to be an expensive failure. The residents had to rely on government checks rather than work.

For the first several years, Eleanor put her own money into the project. She gave presents to the residents each Christmas. She talked to the people and enjoyed potluck dinners and square dances with them. For Eleanor, the fact that she helped transform the lives of hardworking, decent people was a triumph.

FINDING HER PLACE

Throughout Franklin's first term in office, Eleanor established herself as a powerful force in American society. But she and Franklin were very careful that it did not appear that Eleanor was making government policy. They discussed things during informal meetings and at mealtimes. Franklin often loved to bait Eleanor into an argument, just to see how passionate she was about something. Then he would adopt her positions and opinions about a subject as if they had been his own all along.

People in government knew how powerful Eleanor was. Someone with an idea or a proposal for a government program might approach

Eleanor first, to get her excited about the idea. They knew that, if she agreed with something, she would take it directly to the president.

The American people sensed something else in Eleanor. Her compassion and honesty shone through in everything she did. She supported projects that benefited those who most needed help: the poor, the young, mothers and children, working women and men. In her articles, radio addresses, and newspaper columns, she spoke in plain language about the problems and fears that everyone was facing together. People trusted her. But more important, Eleanor trusted them.

Eleanor fought for equality for all Americans; she was especially appalled by the injustices faced by African Americans.

TEN

From Wars at Home to War Abroad

Franklin fought to put into effect government works that would improve the lives of Americans. Between 1933 and 1935, more than a dozen sweeping government programs were established. For instance, the Agricultural Adjustment Act helped farmers. The Civil Works Administration created 4 million public works jobs. The National Youth Administration provided part-time jobs to more than 2 million high school and college students. The Works Progress Administration supported the arts by creating jobs in the theater, fine arts, and literary projects.

Meanwhile, Eleanor was becoming known as someone separate from her husband. This made her feel very proud and confident. "As time went by," she wrote, "I found that people no longer considered me a mouthpiece for my husband but realized that I had a point of view of my own with which he might not at all agree. Then I felt freer to state my views." Franklin continued to rely on her judgment and actively sought her advice, which she was happy to give him.

A GROUP IGNORED

As Eleanor discovered more about the plight of the poor in America, she came face-to-face with the country's worst injustice: the treatment of African Americans. Black people were excluded from restaurants, movie theaters, stores, schools, and hotels. Many employers would not hire blacks for any job. In the South, most blacks could not vote. As Eleanor began to meet and become friends with black leaders, she grew increasingly upset at the treatment of African Americans.

One black leader who became Eleanor's close friend was Mary McLeod Bethune. She and Eleanor met at a luncheon in 1927 and became friends. By the 1930s, Bethune was a regular visitor to the White House.

Many people were shocked and outraged by Eleanor's open acceptance of Bethune and other African Americans. But Eleanor

Eleanor (center) became good friends with Mary McLeod Bethune (left), who Franklin appointed as director of African American affairs in the National Youth Administration.

ignored the criticism. She invited blacks to luncheons and parties at the White House. She visited black schools and communities. She pushed for the New Deal programs to include African Americans and other nonwhite people. By her actions and her words, Eleanor showed

Mary McLeod Bethune

Mary Jane McLeod was born near Maysville, South Carolina, in 1875, the fifteenth of seventeen children. Her parents, Samuel and Patsy Macintosh McLeod, were former slaves. Mary grew up helping on the family farm and then attended a mission school when she was eleven years old. Later, she received a scholarship to Scotia Seminary, a school in North Carolina for African American girls. Mary graduated from Scotia in 1894; then she attended the Moody Bible Institute in Chicago.

In 1904, she started a school for African American students, called the Daytona Literary and Industrial School, in Daytona Beach, Florida. Her extraordinary skills as a teacher, organizer, and fund-raiser allowed her to expand the school. It eventually grew to become Bethune-Cookman College.

Bethune became a respected representative of African Americans through such organizations as the National Council of Negro Women. She organized voter registration drives for African Americans in the face of violence and discrimination. In 1936, Franklin appointed her director of African American affairs in the National Youth Administration. She and Eleanor remained colleagues and close friends for years. Bethune died on May 18, 1955, and was buried on the campus of Bethune-Cookman College.

the country that blacks were human beings who deserved the same respect and opportunities as anyone else.

A SENSE OF IMPENDING DOOM

In Germany, a man named Adolf Hitler and his Nazi Party began to rise to power. In 1933, Hitler became chancellor of Germany, or leader of the national legislature. In 1934, he became president and supreme commander of the armed forces, taking the title Der Führer ("the leader").

Breaking Racism

In 1939, one of the world's greatest singers was an African American named Marian Anderson. She was considered the world's greatest contralto singer during her lifetime. Anderson traveled throughout the world giving concerts. But when she tried to hold a concert at Constitutional Hall in Washington, D.C., she was refused. The Daughters of the American Revolution, a woman's organization that managed the concert hall, would not allow a black person to perform there.

Eleanor was outraged at this blatant show of racism. Anderson was among the greatest singers of all time, and she could not give a concert in Washington, D.C.! Eleanor resigned her membership in the DAR in protest and arranged for Anderson to give a concert on the steps of the Lincoln Memorial on Easter Sunday, April 9, 1939. More than 75,000 people attended the historic concert. The first song that Anderson sang was "America" ("My Country, 'Tis of Thee"), as a symbol of the freedom that she, and all other African Americans, deserved.

Between 1936 and 1940, Hitler's troops invaded and controlled Austria, Czechoslovakia, Poland, Denmark, Norway, France, Belgium, Luxembourg, the Netherlands, Russia, and Romania. The Germans attacked Great Britain, too. Japan and Italy became Germany's allies.

Hitler and the Nazis also set out to destroy the Jewish people. Jewish businesses were closed or demolished. Jewish synagogues were burned. Jews were fired from their jobs. By the end of the 1930s, hundreds of thousands of Jewish people had been forced to flee Europe. Those who didn't escape were put into Nazi work camps.

Americans watched the events unfold in Europe with horror. Publicly, Franklin assured the people that the country would not join the war. Quietly, however, Franklin began making preparations in case war came.

The country was so worried about the war that the Democrats persuaded Franklin, in whose leadership the country had confidence, to run for a third term as president—something no other president had done. He agreed, and he easily won the election of 1940.

In the midst of this unease about war, Eleanor had to deal with two deaths in the family. In September 1941, Sara Roosevelt, Franklin's mother, died. But even more upsetting to Eleanor was the death of her brother, Hall, that same month. Hall had had a troubled life and a failed marriage. He had become an alcoholic like his father and his uncles. Hall was buried at Tivoli, Grandmother Hall's old home. Eleanor was now the only person left in her immediate family.

A bright spot in Eleanor's life was a new friend, Joseph Lash. Lash was a student activist whom Eleanor met in 1939. Although they seemed an unlikely pair—he was in his twenties, and Eleanor was in her fifties—

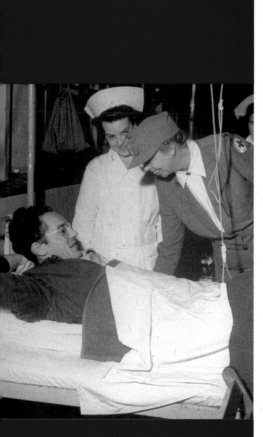

Eleanor visited many wounded soldiers during World War II.

they forged a strong friendship. It was a friendship that Eleanor needed. She and Hick had remained close, but the intensity of their friendship had cooled. In 1938, Eleanor had a falling-out with Nancy Cook and Marion Dickerman. And Franklin, burdened with the pressures of the Great Depression and the oncoming war, became even more remote.

ELEANOR GOES TO WAR

America entered World War II on December 7, 1941, when Japanese planes bombed a naval base in Hawaii called Pearl Harbor. Americans were shocked and terrified. Immediately, Franklin was consumed with the war. Now he and Eleanor saw even less of each other.

Eleanor turned her attention to what she could do for the war effort. During the war, she traveled extensively, visiting places such as Great Britain, the South Pacific, the Caribbean, and Latin America.

One of Eleanor's best-known trips during the war was a 1943 journey to several South Pacific areas, including Australia and New Zealand, to visit wounded soldiers. At first, most of the hardened military officers did not want to bother with a visit from the first lady. But at each stop, she charmed everyone she met. The soldiers' eyes lit up when she spoke to them. They seemed to get better just by having Eleanor among them. One officer wrote later that he marveled at her stamina, both physical and mental. She had a gift for talking to dozens of hospital staff members, orderlies, and soldiers and making each one feel special.

THE END OF MANY THINGS

By 1944, the tide had begun to turn in the war. On June 6, American forces stormed the beaches at Normandy, France. D-Day, as it would be known, signaled that the United States and its allies—including Great Britain, Russia, France, and several other European countries—were winning the war. The American people, and Eleanor, began to hope that the war would soon be over.

Franklin and the Democrats faced yet another presidential election. No president had ever been elected to four terms of office. The strain of the presidency, combined with his general weakness from polio, had taken their toll on Franklin. Eleanor was worried. Franklin and his doctors assured her that he was fine. In November 1944, he was elected to a fourth term in office, the only U.S. president ever to have done so.

The first few months of 1945 saw great victories for the allies. Germany was on the retreat. In February, Franklin traveled to the Russian town of Yalta to meet with Russian leader Joseph Stalin and British Prime Minister Winston Churchill to discuss what would happen to Europe after the war was over.

In March, after he returned from Yalta, Franklin addressed the U.S. Congress. For the first time, he gave a speech sitting down. This made Eleanor very uneasy. She wrote that "I knew . . . that he had accepted a certain degree of invalidism."

On April 12, Eleanor was speaking at a function in Washington when she received an urgent phone call telling her to leave at once. "I did not even ask why," she wrote. "I knew that something dreadful had happened." Franklin had been at Warm Springs for a few days, resting. He was having his portrait painted when he complained of a pain in his head, then collapsed. He died without regaining consciousness.

Eleanor immediately traveled to Warm Springs. When she arrived, she got an even more terrible shock. Lucy Mercer Rutherford, now a widow, had been with Franklin when he died. In fact, the painting he was sitting for was to be a gift for Lucy's daughter.

Eleanor, always careful to hide her emotions, could barely keep herself together as the story of Franklin's last betrayal unfolded. After she

Eleanor and the country mourned Franklin's death.

had heard it all, she silently went into the room where Franklin lay and shut the door. She came out several minutes later, dry-eyed and composed. With great dignity, she began to make funeral arrangements.

Franklin's funeral service drew hundreds of thousands of people. Franklin had guided the country through two of its most terrible times, the Great Depression and World War II. He had shown humor, compassion, and strength. People had felt safe with him. His death was like a physical blow to the country.

Eleanor, too, was devastated. Even though each had found other loves, they had always clung to the hope that one day, they would be romantically close once again. Only a short time before his death, Franklin had confided to their son Elliott that he had wished he could get to know Eleanor better. There had been a bond between them that nothing—not betrayal, not distance, not anger—had ever completely broken. Now it was gone, and Eleanor wasn't sure what to do next.

Though Eleanor and Franklin had problems in their relationship, each was an integral part of the other's life.

ELEVEN

At the End, a New Beginning

After living in the White House for twelve years, Eleanor had to move. In only a few days, she had packed up twelve years' worth of life in the White House and left Washington for good.

Eleanor was surprised at how alone she felt without Franklin. She missed his humor, his judgment, his warm affection, and his strength. Eleanor turned to her close friends, including Hick and Joseph Lash, for comfort. "I want to cling to those I love," she wrote, "because I find that mentally I counted so much on Franklin that I feel a bit bereft."

She had no real idea what she was going to do next. She did know, however, that she wanted to feel useful in some way. And she especially did not want to feel old.

PRIVATE CITIZEN, PUBLIC DELEGATE

Eleanor thought that she could return to private life. But she had become one of the best-known and most respected people in the world. She quickly realized how in-demand she was. During a normal week, Eleanor might receive more than 100 requests for public appearances, but she could accept only a few. For Eleanor, though, "a few" could mean as many as three or four engagements a day.

President Harry S. Truman asked Eleanor to be a delegate for the United States at the first organizational of the United Nations.

She continued to write articles, as well as her newspaper column, "My Day." She gave radio addresses and began work as an editor for the Junior Literary Guild. She was still "Eleanor Everywhere."

In December 1945, President Truman called Eleanor with an idea. A new international organization called the United Nations (UN) had formed after the war. The first organizational of the UN was to be held in early 1946. Would Eleanor like to be one of the five American delegates?

Her first response was to say no. However, after considering it carefully, she finally agreed. Truman was pleased. He knew people would listen to her.

It was an opportunity to work toward a goal that both she and Franklin had shared. "I believed the United Nations to be the one hope for a peaceful world," she wrote. "My husband had placed a great importance on the establishment of this world organization."

A TRIUMPH IN WORLD POLITICS

Not everyone was happy with Truman's choice. Some of her fellow delegates thought that she wouldn't understand the complex procedures of the UN. Without her knowledge, they assigned her to Committee 3, which would handle cultural, educational, and humanitarian issues. They didn't trust her to be on a committee that handled economical or political issues. But she gracefully agreed to serve wherever she was asked.

In fact, Committee 3 became one of the most important committees at the conference. It was given the task of developing plans for millions of war refugees. Some delegates wanted the refugees forcibly returned to their home countries. Others thought that the refugees should live wherever they wanted. The debate lasted well into the night. When it was Eleanor's turn to speak, she talked eloquently about freedom. Although it was very late, everyone stayed to hear her speech. Later, the UN's General Assembly voted against forcing refugees to return to their home countries.

It was a great triumph for Eleanor. She had proven to them all that she could stand up to opposition and defeat it. Few knew that she had been doing this for years, behind the scenes at the White House.

UNIVERSAL HUMAN RIGHTS

After the UN meetings, Eleanor traveled to Europe to see the devastation of the war for herself. The sight shocked her. "I felt that nobody would have imagined such utter, horrible destruction," she wrote.

In 1946, President Truman asked her return to the UN, this time as the U.S. representative on the UN Human Rights Commission. The commission was established to create an international bill of human rights. Eleanor immediately agreed. She held the position for two years, eventually becoming the chairperson of the commission. In addition to this work, she continued to write her columns, give lectures, and appear on radio and television.

Once again, many people at the UN didn't take Eleanor seriously. Now in her sixties, Eleanor didn't look very formidable. She reminded them of a favorite aunt or someone's mother. But those who underestimated Eleanor would soon be surprised. Some called her a "merciless slave driver." If a meeting got unruly, Eleanor could snap the delegates back to the work at hand. By the end of her tenure as chairperson, Eleanor remarked that she had thought raising a large family had tested her patience to its limit. But no, presiding over the commission had been worse!

After two years, the commission finished drafting the Universal Declaration of Human Rights. It laid out a series of rights that every person in the world should have, such as freedom, the right not to be

Eleanor was on the United Nations Human Rights Commission, a group that drafted the Universal Declaration of Human Rights.

The Universal Declaration of Human Rights

The Universal Declaration of Human Rights is not a law. It is a document that lists rules on how to treat people. In the years since it was adopted, it has become extremely important as a standard for international human rights. Many countries have modeled their constitutions after the rights set forth in the declaration. The preamble reads:

Whereas recognition of the inherent dignity and of the equal and inalienable rights of all members of the human family is the foundation of freedom, justice and peace in the world,

Whereas disregard and contempt for human rights have resulted in barbarous acts which have outraged the conscience of mankind, and the advent of a world in which human beings shall enjoy freedom of speech and belief and freedom from fear and want has been proclaimed as the highest aspiration of the common people,

Whereas it is essential, if man is not to be compelled to have recourse, as a last resort, to rebellion against tyranny and oppression, that human rights should be protected by the rule of law,

Whereas it is essential to promote the development of friendly relations between nations,

Whereas the peoples of the United Nations have in the Charter reaffirmed their faith in fundamental human rights, in the dignity and worth of the human person and in the equal rights of men and women and have determined to promote social progress and better standards of life in larger freedom,

Whereas Member States have pledged themselves to achieve, in cooperation with the United Nations, the promotion of universal respect for and observance of human rights and fundamental freedoms,

Whereas a common understanding of these rights and freedoms is of the greatest importance for the full realization of this pledge,

Now, Therefore THE GENERAL ASSEMBLY proclaims THIS UNIVERSAL DECLARATION OF HUMAN RIGHTS as a common standard of achievement for all peoples and all nations, to the end that every individual and every organ of society, keeping this Declaration constantly in mind, shall strive by teaching and education to promote respect for these rights and freedoms and by progressive measures, national and international, to secure their universal and effective recognition and observance, both among the peoples of Member States themselves and among the peoples of territories under their jurisdiction.

tortured or enslaved, and the right not to be discriminated against. On December 10, 1948, the General Assembly voted to adopt it.

The Universal Declaration of Human Rights was one of Eleanor's greatest achievements. She considered it the most important work she ever

Even outside of her activities with the UN, Eleanor continued to be active in politics. In 1960, she spoke in favor of a presidential candidate at the Democratic National Convention.

did. She remained with the UN until 1952, serving on committees or in organizations that supported the UN. Eleanor wrote that she considered the UN to be "the one organization that has the machinery to bring together all nations in an effort to maintain world peace."

NO SLOWING DOWN

During the 1950s, Eleanor stayed busy. She was besieged with offers for speaking engagements and television commercials. And she still wrote her "My Day" column. Eleanor woke up at 7 A.M. each day, made her bed, and exercised before starting her day. She gave more than 100 speeches a year.

In 1960, however, Eleanor began to slow down. A doctor diagnosed her with a blood disease known as aplastic anemia. Two years later, it was discovered that she also had a rare form of tuberculosis centered in her bone marrow. Eleanor knew that it was the end, so she asked to go home to die. About a month later, on November 7, 1962, Eleanor Roosevelt died quietly in her New York City apartment. She was buried next to Franklin in the rose garden of their Hyde Park estate.

ELEANOR'S LEGACY

Eleanor Roosevelt's life began at a time when cars and airplanes had not yet been invented. It ended at the beginning of the Space Age. She lived through the Great Depression and two world wars. In her personal life, she experienced family alcoholism, betrayal, and loss. Through it all, she became one of the most influential people of the twentieth century.

Although she was never elected to public office, she was one of the country's best-known—and in some places, most hated—political figures.

In everything Eleanor did, she achieved a measure of greatness. As the longest-serving first lady in U.S. history, she reinvented the job by living her own life and following her own interests. She worked tirelessly for the American people, no matter what their gender, color, or religion. She fought for equality and justice. In her greatest achievement, the Universal Declaration of Human Rights, she did her best to assure that the basic rights of freedom and happiness would be enjoyed by all people in the world.

But most of all, Eleanor was a woman who had the courage to follow her convictions, even in the face of enormous opposition. "When I feel that I am right in what I do," she wrote, "it seems to me that I cannot afford, as a self-respecting individual, to refuse to do a thing merely because it will make me disliked or bring down a storm of criticism on my head. . . . [W]hen I believe . . . that what I am doing is right I go ahead and try as hard as I can to dismiss from my mind the attitude of those who are hostile. I don't see how else one can live."

Timeline

ELEANOR ROOSEVELT'S LIFE   WORLD EVENTS

1883 Eleanor Roosevelt's parents, Anna Hall and Elliott Roosevelt, are married.

1884 Eleanor is born on October 11.

1892 Eleanor's mother, Anna, dies of diphtheria.

1894 Eleanor's father, Elliott, dies, possibly of a seizure.

1895 The first radio signal is sent and received.

1899–1902 Eleanor attends Allenswood near London, England.

1901 President William McKinley is assassinated and Eleanor's uncle, Theodore Roosevelt, becomes president.

1902 Eleanor "comes out" in society.

The air conditioner is invented.

1903 Eleanor and Franklin secretly become engaged.

The Wright Brothers fly the first airplane.

1905 Eleanor and Franklin marry on March 17.

1906 The Roosevelts' daughter, Anna Eleanor, is born.

1907 The Roosevelts' son James is born.

1908 Henry Ford sells the first Model T automobile.

1909 The Roosevelts' son Franklin Jr. is born; he dies a few months later.

1910 The Roosevelts' son Elliott is born; Franklin becomes a New York state senator.

1912 Eleanor attends her first Democratic Party convention.

1913 Franklin is appointed assistant secretary of the Navy.

1914 The Roosevelts have another son whom they name Franklin Jr.

1916 The Roosevelts' son John is born.

1917 The United States enters World War I.

1918 Eleanor discovers Franklin's affair with Lucy Mercer.

World War I ends.

1920 Eleanor and Louis Howe become friends.

The Nineteenth Amendment is passed, giving women the right to vote.

1921 Franklin contracts polio and is permanently paralyzed.

1922 Eleanor joins the Women's Trade Union League and the Women's Division of the Democratic State Committee; she meets Nancy Cook and Marion Dickerman.

1925 Val-Kill is built in Hyde Park, and the Val-Kill furniture factory is founded.

1926 Eleanor, Nancy, and Marion buy the Todhunter School, and Eleanor begins her teaching career.

1927 Eleanor and Mary McLeod Bethune meet.

Television is invented.

1928 Franklin is elected governor of New York.

Penicillin is discovered.

1929 On October 29, the New York Stock Exchange crashes, beginning the Great Depression.

1932 Franklin is elected president.

1933 Eleanor begins all-women press conferences; the Arthurdale project begins; Franklin launches his New Deal programs.

Adolf Hitler becomes chancellor of Germany.

1934 Hitler becomes Germany's president and armed forces commander.

1935 Eleanor begins publishing her column "My Day."

1936 Franklin wins reelection to the presidency.

1939 Eleanor arranges for contralto Marian Anderson, an African American, to perform at the Lincoln Memorial on April 9.

Hitler invades Poland; war begins in Europe.

The helicopter is invented.

1940 Franklin wins an unprecedented third term to office.

1941 Japanese bomb Pearl Harbor on December 7, the United States enters World War II.

1943 Eleanor goes on a highly publicized tour in the South Pacific to visit U.S. soldiers.

1945 Franklin dies on April 12.

World War II ends on September 2.

1946 Eleanor becomes chairperson of the United Nations Human Rights Commission.

The microwave oven is invented.

1948 The United Nations passes the Universal Declaration of Human Rights.

1952 Eleanor resigns from the United Nations.

1954 The Supreme Court ruling in *Brown vs. the Board of Education* outlaws segregation in public schools.

1957 Congress passes a Civil Rights Act, calling for voting rights for African Americans and paving the way for the broader Civil Rights Act of 1964.

1960 Eleanor supports John F. Kennedy for president; Kennedy is elected.

1962 Eleanor dies on November 7.

To Find Out More

BOOKS

Freedman, Russell. *Eleanor Roosevelt: A Life of Discovery*. New York: Clarion Books, 1997.

Gottfried, Ted. *Eleanor Roosevelt: First Lady of the Twentieth Century*. Danbury, Conn.: Franklin Watts, 1997.

Rosenberg, Pam. *Eleanor Roosevelt*. Minneapolis: Compass Point Books, 2003.

Sawyer, Ken Knapp. *Eleanor Roosevelt*. New York: Dorling Kindersley, 2006.

Thompson, Gare. *Who Was Eleanor Roosevelt?* New York: Grosset & Dunlap, 2004.

VIDEOS

The American Experience: Eleanor Roosevelt. PBS Home Video, 2000.

ORGANIZATIONS AND ONLINE SITES

The American Experience: Eleanor Roosevelt
www.pbs.org/wgbh/amex/Eleanor/index.html

This companion Web site to a documentary about Eleanor's life includes quotes, facts, and information about one of the century's most important women.

Eleanor Roosevelt National Historic Site
www.nps.gov/elro/

This National Park Service site gives a brief description of Val-Kill cottage, which is part of the historic site.

The Eleanor Roosevelt Papers
http://www.gwu.edu/%7Eerpapers/index.html

This Web site gives extensive information on Eleanor's life and her achievements as first lady and as a delegate to the United Nations.

Franklin D. Roosevelt Presidential Library and Museum
www.fdrlibrary.marist.edu

The presidential museum contains a wealth of information about Eleanor, including her papers and dozens of photographs.

Universal Declaration of Human Rights
www.udhr.org

Eleanor considered this document to be her greatest achievement. Here you can read the Declaration and discover its importance as a world document.

A Note on Sources

There is certainly no lack of source materials on Eleanor Roosevelt's life and work. Countless books, articles, speeches, and television programs have exhaustively picked through every aspect of her life. There is an incredible amount of personal, primary source material that she left to history—letters, memos, speeches, private correspondences to family and friends, and thousands of "My Day" columns, as well as magazine articles and books.

But for all of the material that exists, there is much that has disappeared. For instance, before her death, she destroyed Franklin's early letters to her. Much of her correspondence with her close women friends such as Marion Dickerman, Nancy Cook, and Lorena Hickok is gone. While her public life is well documented, her private life remains somewhat veiled, just as it was during her own lifetime.

Over the years, most biographers have subscribed to the popular thought that Eleanor was cold, aloof, and unlovable. They blamed Franklin's failings as a husband on Eleanor's lack of warmth and compassion as a human being. In 1992, biographer Blanche Wiesen Cook created a huge controversy with the first of three installments of her book on Eleanor's life. In the first two volumes, which cover Eleanor's life from 1884 to 1938, Cook dissects Eleanor's relationship with Franklin and theorizes that their problems were due as much to Franklin's inattention as to Eleanor's inability to get close to him. Cook also suggests that Eleanor may have had lesbian relationships with some of her friends, most notably Lorena Hickok. She also puts forth the idea that Eleanor had a long-term romantic relationship with her bodyguard, Earl Miller.

While none of these theories can be proven with certainty, the mere suggestion that Eleanor could have had a rich sexual life outside her marriage—and the possibility of relationships with other women—caused an uproar. Roosevelt biographers dismissed Cook's conclusions, supplying their own proof against the allegations. Without the letters and private correspondence between Eleanor and these people, we will never know for sure. But Cook's theories suggest that Eleanor was a much deeper, more emotional and thoughtful woman than many had previously thought. Cook's work and the dozens of more traditional tellings of Eleanor's life offer a comprehensive picture of a sometimes surprisingly deep woman who is considered to be one of the greatest Americans who ever lived.

— Allison Lassieur

Bibliography

BOOKS

Asbell, Bernard. *Mother and Daughter: The Letters of Eleanor and Anna Roosevelt.* New York: Coward, McCann & Geoghegan, 1982.

Black, Allida M., ed. *Courage in a Dangerous World: The Political Writings of Eleanor Roosevelt.* New York: Columbia University Press, 1999.

Caroli, Betty Boyd. *The Roosevelt Women.* New York: Basic Books, 1998.

Collier, Peter. *The Roosevelts: An American Saga.* New York: Simon & Schuster, 1994.

Cook, Blanche Wiesen. *Eleanor Roosevelt: Volume 1, 1884–1933.* New York: Viking, 1992.

— *Eleanor Roosevelt: Volume 2, 1933–1939.* New York: Viking, 1999.

Goodwin, Doris Kearns. *No Ordinary Time. Franklin and Eleanor Roosevelt: The Home Front in World War II.* New York: Simon & Schuster, 1994.

Hareven, Tamara K. *Eleanor Roosevelt: An American Conscience.* Chicago: Quadrangle Books, 1968.

Roosevelt, David B. *Grandmere: A Personal History of Eleanor Roosevelt.* New York: Warner Books, 2002.

Roosevelt, Eleanor. *You Learn by Living.* New York: Harper & Brothers, 1960.

— *The Autobiography of Eleanor Roosevelt.* New York: Harper & Brothers, 1960.

Scharf, Lois. *Eleanor Roosevelt: First Lady of American Liberalism.* Boston: Twayne Publishers, 1987.

Youngs, J. William T. *Eleanor Roosevelt: A Personal and Public Life.* New York: Little, Brown & Co., 1985.

Index

About the Author

Allison Lassieur has written more than seventy books about famous figures, historical subjects, world cultures, current events, and science. In addition to writing, Lassieur studies medieval textile history. She lives in Pennsylvania in a 100-year-old house with her husband, Charles.